Muir

All rights reserved; no part of this book may be reproduced by any means without the publisher's permission.

ISBN: 978-1-913642-81-5

The author has asserted their right to be identified as the author of this Work in accordance with the Copyright, Designs and Patents Act 1988

Book designed by Aaron Kent

Edited by Aaron Kent

Broken Sleep Books (2021), Talgarreg, Wales

Contents

Crab Snowglobe	7
Vatersay	8
The animal that never was	9
giant	10
Palindrome	12
Bicycle	13
The dog bat	14
Ruth	16
Vegetarian	17
Lunch	18
Seven Postcards	19
Enxaneta	21
Tornadoes	22
Second Time in Mexico City	23
Up your street	24
Tuesday	25
Pylon	26
Anecdote with dogs	27
Friday	28
Forrest Gump	29
Acknowledgements	31

New Year's Eve

Annie Muir

Crab Snowglobe

Thrown in with shoelaces and paracetamol,
a souvenir from Copson Street pound shop –

this rusty orange crab on a rock
with specks of glitter resting

in every nook and cranny.
Around the base there are footprints in sand

and another, smaller crab,
exactly alike except I can touch it.

Inside your hard, glass globe
you seem to be in some other dimension

like the reflection in a mirror,
or memory.

Either dormant or ecstatic –
when I shake you up

it is for a moment New Year's Eve,
your pincers grasping to catch the confetti

that floats around your head
in kaleidoscope slow motion.

Then, when each piece has fallen, you wait
for something else to happen.

Vatersay

I grew up here in another life
in a white house full of brothers and sisters

We used to watch planes landing on the beach
Mum had long hair then cut it short

I came here to think about my self
but all I can think about is him

A man on the beach who looks washed up
packing bits of rubbish into a plastic bag

I walk uphill through fields of purple clover
towards a big abandoned house

The same man welcomes me, takes my coat –
drops it to the floor

offers me champagne – an old boot
introduces me to his wife – a pile of bricks

and invites me to dinner – I can only imagine
what's on the menu

I politely decline and walk back outside
pretending to close the door behind me

I've been coming here since I was a child
Me and Katie left food out for the fairies

and woke up to a thank you note in fairy handwriting
I wrote the note and even fooled myself

The animal that never was
after Rilke

The animal was strange and new,
but still they tried to love its patterned neck,
its clown feet, its mute eyes.

It wasn't real, but they loved it so it was,
and it smiled. They gave it a room
with a bed and some books and it read
and read and forgot about trying

to be. They fed it coco pops
and questions until its forehead
was so full of sugar and words

that it grew a horn. A single horn.
And when it looked hard into the silver mirror
it saw nothing but the pale slate
of a young girl's face.

giant

(after a painting by leonora carrington)

friends stop

growing, stop

catching your eye

or the giggles, size twelve

boots burst at the toes you start

to get the picture, catch your ankle

swingers in the mirror, frizzy mane tinted

by rain, eyes that seemed huge in childhood

rendered foreign plug sockets. you are growing up

away from grass and greens, trees like little puffs of smoke

to stub your toes on, bony birds look uglier up-close, use you

for shelter. parents tell you to be patient, tie long plaits down your back

to anchor you, have no idea you can see further than their short-sighted aphorisms,

in april you can smell the winter snow, your toes tucked into earth can feel toilets spinning

backwards in new zealand, you hear the clouds sneeze, have already designed your own plaque for

the natural history museum, chosen a place next to the bones of the big blue whale, you know you are

lucky really, never had bedbugs, lulled to sleep by swinging cranes, only kept awake by stars and planes.

Palindrome

She ate her breakfast backwards, *crunch*,
spitting toast back on the plate and scraping butter off.
She got into bed and slept, woke up,
and went to the pub. All her friends were there –
shouldn't they be at work? –
she couldn't understand what anyone said
but acted like she could. A man with black hair
sat outside. He talked with his hands so was easier to hear
and he conjured cigarettes from ashtrays.
She went to the library and pretended to read
from back to front like Japanese,
went home and ate her breakfast, *crunch*,
got into bed, slept, woke up, picked up her phone
and it rang – *MUM* – she answered and it sounded like

the end of the world. She tried to ignore
reversing cars and dust and hair clinging
to her body. She closed her eyes and saw
a photo: of her mum, dad, brother, sister, her,
and an inflatable killer whale, in a swimming pool,
treading water. *Children are time made solid*,
her mother said, *atomic clocks…*
Atoms weren't supposed to split up, so it was a shock
when they did. The children were all teenagers by then
and not very solid – her mother hung up
and she tried to hold on to the image. A black hair
from the floor landed on her shoulder and she brushed it
away. She tried to remember what happened the night before,
she only drank two pints of *1864*.

Bicycle

My mum gave me her old one
and I sat by it on the train

as if it were a sleeping baby in a pram
as I whizzed away from the womb again.

She used it to cycle around France and Spain
before I was born. Hard to imagine

her who does the crossword every day
with long hair, middle parted,

racing downhill in the middle of nowhere –
then, she must have found it hard

to imagine giving it away
to her middle child who now

sits in a waiting room
looking a pair of glasses in the eye.

The optician says my name and I jump
and read letters from a glowing page

until I can't anymore. My eyes have got worse.
As I go to stop at the first red light

the brakes on my bike honk
like a sad goose.

The dog bat

Torch-lit mouth open
as if telling a scary story
round a bonfire,

you are an abandoned
inside-out umbrella
on a windy rainy day,

an umbrella made of tiny bones.
Wings hang from your neck,
wrapped around

like a towel,
like trying to hide
something.

Flat-chested, cleaving to the stump
like to a body or bed
but looking up

at a potential threat
or a possible future –
a much-needed change of scene?

Chihuahua-head, ears pricked
like at the jangle of a lead.
A look of shock in the shiny eyes,

a look of seeing something
that goes against everything
you've seen so far,

like a painting of Paris
when all you've seen
are the streets of Blackness,

a look of hearing
about your death, or
about how after death

you'll be stuffed in a museum
surrounded by blind moles
and a hedgehog.

Ruth

We stood on a bridge
and a train went under
our legs. We waved
and the driver
beeped. We endured
rivers and barbed-wire
because Ruth said
ten people a year are killed
by charging cows. We saw
Mam Tor bus stop.

The top was windy. We got a photo.

I chased Ruth down
pretending to be
a cow. We hitched back
with two old men listening
to classical music who said
our little legs must be
exhausted.

Vegetarian

All men are pigs, even the best of them
was a joke or warning my mum gave to me,

and her mum gave the same to her, she said,
and her mum gave the same to her. I snorted –

and left to go and see the new Macbeth.
Tears the size of babies' heads rolled down the cheeks

of actors – men and women born of men
and women. I looked around:

the cinema was full. I squeezed through crowds of bodies, then
I went and wolfed a sweating bacon roll.

Lunch

Rose told me not to be afraid
of colour, and I thought of that woman
eating at her desk, scrolling through holiday websites.

Now when I walk around at lunchtime
I go to the supermarket and look
at all the red and yellow,

the ready meals and half price meat,
get lost amongst rows
and rows of shelves of tins, boxes, bags, bottles

arranged in lines. I pick up a carton of orange juice
and behind is another identical to it.
I walk down the aisle with my choices in hand

and stand in the queue and look at the magazines
Closer and *Now* – I get to the front
and am sent to self-checkout which addresses me

familiarly, like an answer phone message
from a wrong number.
I go and eat my sandwich in the art gallery

standing in front of 'The Dinner Hour' –
mill girls with their clogs and shawls and aprons...
Back at the office she is sitting there, still.

Seven Postcards
for Amber

The headrest on the plane said: 'Have a nice time here, you are nearly there.' Here there are buses called FINNAIR and the metro looks like a cave, with chalk-white mooses on the walls. We've seen singing policemen perform, and found a message scribbled on the red bricks of an empty factory: 'I was here in 1967'. I'm feeling seasick. See you soon

Through the hostel window I can see a woman wrapped in a duvet – it's next-door to a strip club. Yesterday we learnt about the Baltic Way and walked down tired roads and followed a girl drawing her dog into the shallow sea. At dusk we watched tower blocks from a rock, my teeth chattered and Elton John sang don't let the sun go down on me. See you soon

Today we saw peeling buildings and I bought a second-hand pink flower print dress. You might not like it. An old woman helped me zip up the back in the toilet queue and smiled as if she knew. We dressed up a naked statue in our clothes. All the patterns here make me want to live somewhere else. See you soon

We are trapped indoors because it's raining. In a little art shop a man asked us if we wanted to see "seven paintings about feelings?" and then he went through them one by one: "this one's pain, you know, when someone hurts you, you feel pain? This one's anger, you know, when someone hurts you…" This card is 'tears', I bought it for seven litas. See you soon

I can't move but soon I will have to catch a train. Last night we went to a bar with damp red fur on the walls and a man told us a story about his two front teeth. He said they were fake because once his mum was on the phone and he was nagging for her to change the channel so she threw the remote to him and it knocked them both out. See you soon

I am in the town where Miffy was born. We bumped into someone from our old secondary school who's starting university here, and we found a wine shop with his name so we sprawled outside it on a bench with a silver cat, and made a comic strip where the cat evolves into a human. There are frogs in our hostel's garden that bleep like digital watches. See you soon

I have been here before. My parents asked me if I wanted to go to Anne Frank's house or a houseboat museum and I chose the houseboat. So I went this time to make up for my wrong decision. She had cut out pictures from newspapers and pasted them onto the walls: Greta Garbo, Elizabeth of York and a chimpanzee tea party. See you soon

Enxaneta

In Barcelona it is 38 degrees
and a little girl screams with mimicked joy –

she is all eyelashes, all eyes,
all teeth and gums and tongue.

I hate her through the eyes of her big sister:
half a plastic broken heart tied around my neck,

I climb a fence to watch the *castellers*.
They huddle, arms up as if reaching for a throat,

others climb them like stairs, feet clinging to backs
like tadpoles on their first legs,

it doesn't stop, more like ants than people
but with muscle and bone and white trousers,

two little girls heading for top,
one takes her place below, the other

is no longer a child but the star
at the top of a Christmas tree,

her arm pointing up is the man on the moon,
a clock striking midnight on New Year's Eve.

She slides down the legs of her supporters,
relieving the mountains of tension from their shoulders.

Tornadoes

In an air-conditioned bus you told me about your mum
and your cat called something that means something in Korean

and said you would know
when you found the person you want to marry.

I said I wouldn't, would always think there was someone better,
but you said you would

and it sounded final so I left it there
and fell asleep. You said I missed a good view of cactuses.

In a winding *colectivo* you told me about your pick-up truck
and all the tornadoes back home.

It felt strange not to hear a loud voice in the background
wherever I went, and when I saw a Scotia Bank

I looked away. On *dia de los muertos* I thought of you
and all your brothers and sisters, and your dad, who all left Kansas.

In an air-conditioned bus I sat next to a stranger
and saw the view you'd seen while I had slept.

Second Time in Mexico City

I wake up on a bus to men selling pink afros and puppies
to stopped traffic. This city is a giant market

and I am staying in the electronics section.
But here in this park I'm glad to see

that the clock on the fountain is wrong
and a little boy shouts ¡*adios agua!* as he passes.

I find an indoor flower market where an old man
trims the stalk of a red rose

and I carry it up five flights of stairs
to this rooftop where I watch the sun set again

and think of a poem recited to me
by a middle-aged man on a bench in Oaxaca –

when I planted rose bushes I always grew roses.

There are lights going on and off in apartment blocks
and a woman ironing.

The city stands tall around me like a wall of footballers
holding their crotches. Don't go out at night –

just come up here and watch planes radiate the city
landing one after another

like flies getting caught in a venus fly trap.

Up your street

I have no idea how everything works
but somehow I stay up.

When a car beeps a carbon copy of me
floats out of my body like losing a life

and my real body vibrates like a two-pronged fork
in Science. Once, I fell off –

my first day, poems filled my bag
which swung into the wheel

and my real body somersaulted
over the carbon copy and landed

in the road. A woman in nurse's uniform
jumped out of her car shouting: "I'm not a nurse! I'm not a nurse!"

and gave me a lift to the walk-in centre.
I was only fifteen minutes late in the end

with a big plaster on my elbow.
My new classmates laughed and asked me what happened.

Tuesday

They should have said: it's not bad to feel so deeply,
hermanita, you just have to learn not to spill. On the table
next to mine a woman decides whether or not to
keep her baby, and my stomach rumbles
reminding me my mum was born today and it's too late
to send a card, and her disappointment is my own
and all the choices I've ever made have been wrong.
Is it because I moved five minutes down the road
and my head hasn't caught up with my body yet
like those children's books where you turn the flaps to change the outfits,
or is there something else I haven't thought of? I accidentally
buy banana flavoured baby teething gel for my ulcers, which tastes
really nice but doesn't work, and it comes to me unstoppably
like a sneeze. I laugh as my body clicks painfully into place.

Pylon

She stands by the lake
like the ribcage of a dinosaur.

A spider's web for catching clouds
with six arms like a god or six legs like a bug.

She is pear shaped,
the capital A at the start of the alphabet,

caged in her steel corset dress
and barbed wire socks. A puppeteer of seagulls

managing the ducks that sprinkle her lake
like hundreds and thousands on a 99

but also a puppet herself, held up by wires
like lines indicating movement –

she is the shed skin of a moment in your life. A monument
to the here and now

like a photo of you with a different haircut
or a pair of old shoes

tied to your new ones by the laces
but trailing behind, covered in mud.

Anecdote with dogs

A week later I see them still –
silhouettes, couples mostly,

walking their dogs along the Mersey.
And disappearing with every step, becoming nondescript,

they may as well be ghosts
in slow aperture photos.

While I without dog seem worth noting
somewhere in the back of the mind.

I take off my shoe to inspect a growing blister
and watch a large dog frighten a little girl

who screams and hides behind her father's legs,
but the dog just peers around the bend and she screams again.

My dogs don't frighten her
(I do have a few, now I think about it)

she sees right through them to the juicy bones
that she feels in her own shoulders, knees and toes.

My dogs are glued to my side, the first things people notice,
the few words I speak to strangers on a solo outing –

excuse me, excuse me, thank you,
excuse me, yes please, thank you.

Friday

It's a lovely story, they said
when they called me from the paper,
can you tell us what happened?

What happened was I woke up to find
him outside my front door and named him Bobbie.
It's a lovely story, they said.

I bought some food and Bobbie ate
then fell asleep in the sun on my lap
while I thought of what should happen next.

Later I found out his name really *was* Bobbie,
and he'd travelled a distance of five miles to find me.
It is a lovely story, they said.

'Works in the art gallery,' they said, 'writes poetry'
but not that I guessed his name was Bobbie
when they wrote about what happened.

The owners were 'over the moon', they said,
three young kids had missed their Bobbie.
It is a very lovely story,
hard to believe it really happened to me.

Forrest Gump

I remember my mum asking me if I'd
made him watch Forrest Gump yet?

about some boyfriend. And it's true.
It never gets old. I don't even remember

the first time I watched it.
I think it was at Ellie's house.

She had a huge DVD collection
and told me how they used old footage,

adding in Tom Hanks to make it seem real,
and I thought that's so clever. But Ellie is clever.

And it never gets old. Every time I watch it
I'm connected to all the others

watching it, and crying, if not all the way through,
at least at the end when he talks to Jenny's grave.

This time it was before she'd even offered him
a seat on the bus. I know it's cheesy

but I think there's something in it – that way of love
apart. You are not with the person you love

but you think of them whenever you see something nice
or sad, and they're thinking of you too

even though you never really know if they actually are
until one day they tell you

when you're on your deathbed: *you were (with me).*
It never gets old. And I never get old.

I just keep starting again from scratch, from square one, from Good Morning! from Happy New Year!

Acknowledgements

With thanks to *The Moth*, *The Poetry Bus Magazine*, *Dreich, Sand Journal*, *datableed* and *Pylon of the Month*, where some of these poems have previously appeared. 'Seven Postcards' won the PBS National Student Poetry Competition in 2013, chosen by Daljit Nagra, in which 'The animal that never was' was also a runner up. Thanks to my tutors at Manchester, Vona Groarke and John McAuliffe. Thanks to my family and friends, to Laia, and to Harley.

LAY OUT YOUR UNREST

CPSIA information can be obtained
at www.ICGtesting.com
Printed in the USA
BVHW041745240321
603339BV00005B/634